How to Draw the Life and Times of
Thomas Jefferson

Melody S. Mis

The Rosen Publishing Group's
PowerKids Press™
New York

To Jim and Carol Ochs for letting me be your oldest daughter

Published in 2006 by The Rosen Publishing Group, Inc.
29 East 21st Street, New York, NY 10010

First Edition

Editor: Jennifer Way
Layout Design: Julio A. Gil

Illustrations: All illustrations by Holly Cefrey
Photo Credits: p. 4 Independence National Historical Park; p. 7 © Bettmann/Corbis; p. 8 Colonial Williamsburg Foundation; p. 9 © William Manning/Corbis; p. 10,14 Monticello/Thomas Jefferson Foundation, Inc; p. 12 © David Muench/Corbis; p. 16 © Private Collection/Bridgeman Art Library; p. 18 Library of Congress Prints and Photographs Division; pp. 20, 28 © Burstein Collection/Corbis; p. 22 (top) © José F. Poblete/Corbis; p. 22 (bottom) © Buddy Mays/Corbis; p. 24 © Courtesy of Oregon Historical Society, Portland, OrHi 101540; p. 26 © Joseph Sohm; ChromoSohm Inc/Corbis.

Library of Congress Cataloging-in-Publication Data

Mis, Melody S.
How to draw the life and times of Thomas Jefferson / Melody S. Mis.— 1st ed.
   p. cm. — (A kid's guide to drawing the presidents of the United States of America)
Includes bibliographical references and index.
ISBN 1-4042-2980-9 (lib. bdg.)
1. Jefferson, Thomas, 1743–1826—Juvenile literature. 2. Presidents—United States—Biography—Juvenile literature. 3. Drawing—Technique—Juvenile literature. I. Title. II. Series.

E332.79.M55 2006
973.4'6'092—dc22

2004013475TK

Manufactured in the United States of America

Contents

Thomas Jefferson

Thomas Jefferson is an important figure in U.S. history. He wrote the Declaration of Independence and served as the country's third president. Jefferson was also an inventor and an architect.

Jefferson was born on April 13, 1743, at Shadwell, near Charlottesville, Virginia. His mother, Jane Randolph, came from a wealthy Virginian family. His father, Peter, was a farmer. He owned slaves, who worked on the Shadwell farm.

When Jefferson was 16 years old, he entered the College of William and Mary in Williamsburg, Virginia. He spent two years in college and then studied law for five years.

In 1769, Jefferson was elected to the Virginia legislature. One year after his election, Jefferson began building Monticello, his home, near Charlottesville. In 1772, he married Martha Wayles Skelton.

In 1775, during the American Revolution, Jefferson left the legislature to attend a meeting of the 13 colonies in Philadelphia, Pennsylvania. In 1776, Jefferson was asked to write a document that became known as the Declaration of Independence.

Jefferson served as governor of Virginia from 1779 to 1781. In 1784, Jefferson went to France to make trade agreements with other countries. He returned to the United States in 1789, and became George Washington's secretary of state. The secretary of state deals with relations between the United States and other countries. In 1797, Jefferson was elected vice president. Four years later, Jefferson was elected the third president of the United States.

You will need the following supplies to draw the life and times of Thomas Jefferson:

✓ A sketch pad   ✓ An eraser   ✓ A pencil   ✓ A ruler

These are some of the shapes and drawing terms you need to know:

Horizontal Line	——	Squiggly Line	∿
Oval	⬭	Trapezoid	⏢
Rectangle	▭	Triangle	△
Shading	▓	Vertical Line	|
Slanted Line	/	Wavy Line	∿

The Third President

In 1801, Thomas Jefferson became the nation's third president and the first president to be inaugurated in the new capital city of Washington, D.C. During his presidency, Jefferson lived in the White House, which was still under construction.

Jefferson accomplished many things during his eight years in office. He cut the military's spending and reduced taxes. Jefferson's most important accomplishment during his presidency was doubling the size of the United States by purchasing the Louisiana Territory. In 1803, Jefferson paid France $15 million for land that stretched from the Mississippi River to the Rocky Mountains. The next year he sent Meriwether Lewis and William Clark to explore the new territory. Their journey is called the Voyage of Discovery. Lewis and Clark wrote in their diaries about the plants, animals, rivers, mountains, and Native Americans that they saw on their journey. This news attracted people to move to the new territory and establish settlements.

In this painting by Clyde Osmer de Land, Jefferson *(right)* is shown working on an early draft of the Declaration of Independence with Benjamin Franklin *(left)*.

Jefferson's Virginia

Tuckahoe Plantation *(above)* is a national historic landmark.

Virginia

Map of the United States of America

Thomas Jefferson lived most of his life in Virginia, and many of the homes that he lived in are still standing today. When Jefferson was two years old, his family moved to Tuckahoe Plantation, a large farm 50 miles (80 km) from Shadwell. Jane Randolph Jefferson's cousin William Randolph, the plantation's owner, had died and left four small children. The Jeffersons moved to Tuckahoe to take care of the Randolph children. This plantation would be Jefferson's home for the next seven years. This house is used today for special events.

The most famous monument to Thomas Jefferson is the Thomas Jefferson Memorial in Washington, D.C.

John Russell Pope designed the memorial in 1936. President Franklin Delano Roosevelt opened the memorial to the public in 1943, on the two-hundredth anniversary of Jefferson's birth.

The Jefferson Memorial is 129 feet (39 m) high and weighs 32,000 tons (29,030 t). It is made of limestone and marble. Inside the memorial is a 19-foot (6 m) bronze statue of Jefferson that was designed by Rudolph Evans. The grounds of the memorial are planted with Japanese cherry trees and flowers that are native to Virginia.

The Jefferson Memorial *(above)* in Washington, D.C., is the most famous memorial to Thomas Jefferson.

Jefferson and Music

Music was one of Thomas Jefferson's favorite hobbies, and it played an important role in his life. As a young man Jefferson learned how to play the violin. It was common for gentlemen in the eighteenth century to learn how to play an instrument as part of their education. Jefferson bought his first violin in 1768 and practiced playing it every day for 3 hours. By the time Jefferson went to college, he played the violin very well. In fact, while he was in college, he was often invited to play for dinner parties at the Governor's Palace in Williamsburg.

Playing music was a hobby that Jefferson and his wife, Martha, shared. Martha played the harpsichord. A harpsichord looks like a small piano. It has wire strings that are plucked, or pulled with the fingers. Martha and Jefferson often sang and played musical pieces together in the parlor at Monticello. The Jefferson children also learned to play musical instruments, including the harpsichord and the guitar.

1

You are going to draw Jefferson's harpsichord, which can be seen at Monticello. Use a ruler to help draw the rectangle and the slanted shape.

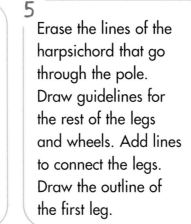

2

Draw three lines to make the top of the harpsichord. Add three lines to the side. Erase the line between the two shapes you drew in step 1.

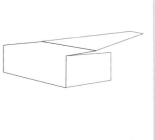

3

Draw the two straight lines to finish the side of the harpsichord. Above the shapes you have drawn add the shape as shown. This part of the harpsichord closes to protect the strings.

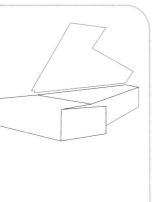

4

Draw the pole that holds up the top cover. Add straight lines to the front. Use a ruler to help draw a guideline for the first leg. Draw a small circle for the wheel.

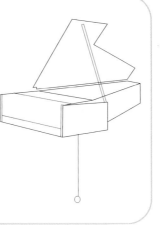

5

Erase the lines of the harpsichord that go through the pole. Draw guidelines for the rest of the legs and wheels. Add lines to connect the legs. Draw the outline of the first leg.

6

Draw the outlines for the remaining legs and for the connecting bars. Well done!

7

Erase the guidelines. Draw the small shapes near the front left leg. Add detail lines to the front of the harpsichord. Add small rectangles for keys.

8

Finish with shading. Notice that the cover is dark and the area for the strings is light.

The Natural Bridge

The Natural Bridge is located in western Virginia. In the eighteenth and nineteenth centuries, it was a popular attraction for European visitors when they traveled to the United States. When Thomas Jefferson saw the bridge in its beautiful setting, he fell in love with it. In 1774, Jefferson bought

157 acres (63.5 ha) of land, which included the bridge, from George III, king of England. He built a small cabin on the property so guests could visit and see the bridge. The bridge is a 90-foot- (27 m) wide arch that rises 215 feet (65.5 m). It was formed of limestone more than 100 million years ago. The Monacan Native Americans, who once lived in the area, called it the Bridge of God. In 1833, Jefferson's family sold the Natural Bridge and the surrounding property to help pay Jefferson's debts. Today the Natural Bridge is a national historic landmark and remains a popular travel spot.

1

To begin the Natural Bridge, draw the squiggly lines as shown. These lines make one side of the bridge's walls.

2

Draw more squiggly lines as shown. These lines make the other side of the bridge.

3

Draw more squiggly lines as shown. These lines form the "bridge" in the Natural Bridge. It is called a bridge because of the narrow band of rock that connects the larger rocks on either side.

4

Draw trees and bushes along the top of the bridge. Draw rocks along the ground and in the pond. Draw a small tree near the arch of the bridge.

5

Add squiggly lines all over the rocks. Add a small bush on the rocks on the left. Draw one more large squiggly line under the bridge.

6

Draw small curvy lines for grass and squiggles inside the tree tops. Finish with detailed shading. The underside of the arch is very dark.

Monticello

Monticello is one of America's most beautiful homes. The name Monticello means "little mountain" in Italian. Thomas Jefferson began building this home in 1770. Jefferson enjoyed studying architecture and using his knowledge to construct and improve buildings. He spent the next 40 years changing and rebuilding the home to look like it does today.

Jefferson based Monticello on the Classical Revival style. This style of architecture uses features such as columns and rounded arches that were found on ancient Roman and Greek buildings. After having lived in France, Jefferson rebuilt part of Monticello to include French architectural features, such as the dome. He added some of his own inventions, including a dumbwaiter. A dumbwaiter is a small elevator that carries objects between floors. The grounds at Monticello are divided into farmland, flower gardens, and an orchard. Today Monticello is a historic location that is open to the public.

1

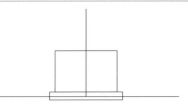

Use a ruler to draw a horizontal line. Draw a vertical line at the center of the horizontal line. Draw a long, thin rectangle that goes over the middle of the horizontal line. Draw a rectangle on top of that.

5

Erase the extra lines. Add an arching window and two lines inside the triangle. Add more shapes to the roof as shown. Draw a triangle above the door. Draw the four windows. Add tops to the columns. Erase extra lines.

2

Erase the lines that run through the long, thin rectangle. Draw two V's near the ends of the rectangle. Draw the shapes as shown to make the front of Monticello. Add the lines to the top center rectangle.

6

Add more windows using arches and rectangles. Add lines to the window you drew in step 5. Begin to draw the dome on the roof. Draw the fence and posts on each side of the the roof.

3

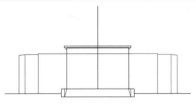

Add more sections to the building. Draw horizontal lines near the tops of the shapes from step 2. Draw two lines to make a large triangle on top of the center rectangle. Draw four columns in the center rectangle.

7

Finish the dome. Add three arching windows to it. Add triangles to the fence shapes on the roof. Draw lines in the arching center window. Add two smaller columns behind the two outer columns. Add more windows.

4

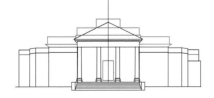

Draw lines in the horizontal rectangle to make stairs. Add bottoms to the columns. Add the shapes and lines to the top of the building and to the tops of the side sections. Draw a small rectangle for the front door.

8

Erase the center guideline. Finish with detailed shading. The shutters are dark. Use the side of your pencil tip to shade in the front of the building. Shade dark and light lines as shown.

The Declaration of Independence

During the American Revolution, which lasted from 1775 to 1783, Thomas Jefferson attended meetings of the Continental Congress in Philadelphia, Pennsylvania. Congress was made up of people from the colonies who were unhappy with British rule  and wanted the colonies to become an independent country. In June 1776, Congress selected a committee to write a document to send to King George III. The document listed the reasons the colonists wanted to be free from British rule and to establish their own government.

The 33-year-old Jefferson spent 17 days writing the Declaration of Independence. He based the declaration on the idea that all men are created equal and that they have the right to life, liberty, and the pursuit of happiness. The Declaration of Independence was approved by Congress on July 4, 1776. In the United States, this day is celebrated as a national holiday known as Independence Day.

1

Begin by drawing the rectangular chair seat and the oval tabletop. The right leg of the table cannot be seen, so you do not need to draw it.

2

Draw curvy shapes for the table legs. Use straight lines to make the sides of the tabletop. Add lines to make the legs of the chair. Draw a stick figure using straight lines and an oval for the head.

3

Erase the guidelines for the table. Draw two more stick figures as shown. Notice the positions of their arms and legs.

4

Add ovals to help you shape the arms, legs, hands, and feet on all three figures. From left to right these figures will be Ben Franklin, John Adams, and Thomas Jefferson.

5

Draw the clothing and body outlines for Franklin and Jefferson. Draw the hands. Draw the papers in the hands. Each figure has papers in one hand.

6

Erase the body guidelines. Draw the body outline and clothes on Adams. Draw a back to Franklin's chair. Draw papers on the table and a pen as shown. Draw feather pens as shown.

7

Erase the body guidelines on the third figure. Erase the lines of the table that run through the papers. Draw the shoes as shown. Add details to the clothing. Draw the faces and hair as shown.

8

Erase the remaining guide ovals. Finish with shading, noting which areas are the darkest. Use the side of your pencil tip to shade the floor and underneath the table.

Jefferson and Religious Freedom

The American colonies were tied to the Church of England, which was renamed the Episcopal Church after the American Revolution. In the eighteenth century, it was common for a country or a state to be united with

a church. The people's taxes supported the church, even if they did not attend this church.

Thomas Jefferson tried to secure Virginians the right to worship as they pleased. He argued that church and state should be separate. He wrote the Bill for Establishing Religious Freedom in 1777. With the help of his friend and fellow legislator James Madison, Jefferson was able to pass the bill in the state legislature in 1786, when he was governor of Virginia. When Jefferson became governor in 1779, the Governor's Palace in Williamsburg served as his home. The capital of Virginia was changed from Williamsburg to Richmond in 1780. The Governor's Palace, shown above, still stands today and is part of the popular Colonial Williamsburg historic area.

1

You will draw the Governor's Palace in Williamsburg. Use your ruler to draw a large rectangle. Draw two horizontal lines at the bottom as shown.

2

Draw three lines for the center front of the palace. Draw a roof edge on top. Add two vertical rectangles for the gateposts.

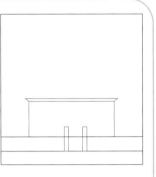

3

Add trapezoids to the tops of the gateposts. Erase the lines that run between and through the gateposts. Add three lines to make a trapezoid with the line you drew in step 2. Draw horizontal lines as shown.

4

Add shapes to the gateposts. Draw the shapes between the posts. Add windows. Some of the window rectangles overlap with the guides. Draw two chimneys. Draw another horizontal guideline.

5

Erase extra lines. Draw steps in the shape between the gateposts. Draw lines to make the door. Draw the tower on the roof as shown. Add details to the roof, including windows.

6

Erase the window guideline on the roof. Add triangular shapes to the outer two windows. Add the lines to the chimneys. Add to the shapes on the tower. Draw vertical lines along the top of the roof.

7

Add detail to the tower and the windows. Add points to two more roof windows. Add a door and balcony on the second story. Draw details on the gate and the horizontal lines on either side of the gate.

8

Finish with detailed shading. You have finished drawing the Governor's Palace.

The Great Collaboration

Thomas Jefferson and James Madison were friends for 50 years. They were both from Virginia, where Madison was born in 1751. The two men shared political ideas and often worked together. From 1776 to 1779, both men served in the Virginia legislature. Jefferson and Madison proposed laws that gave the people of Virginia more freedom and equality. Their work together is called the Great Collaboration. Collaboration means working together.

Madison used many ideas that he had talked about with Jefferson when he wrote the Bill of Rights for the U.S. Constitution in 1791. The Bill of Rights outlines the rights of U.S. citizens. Madison also wrote portions of the Constitution, and for this he is known as the Father of the Constitution. Jefferson would later choose Madison to be secretary of state in 1801. In 1808, Madison would be elected the fourth president of the United States. James Madison died in 1836.

1

You are going to draw James Madison. Begin by drawing a large rectangle. Draw an oval guideline for the head. Draw a line for the center of the body.

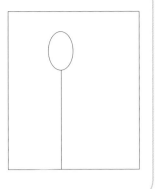

2

Draw a curved line on the side of the head oval. Draw a line for the shoulders. Add a table shape in the left corner.

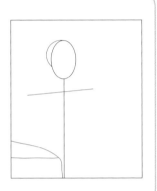

3

Draw guidelines for the eyes, nose, and mouth. Draw a small curvy line for the ear. Draw guidelines and ovals for the arms and hands.

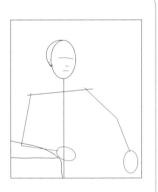

4

Draw the body outline as shown. On the right draw the side of the chair and its arm. The arm is made by stacking three round shapes.

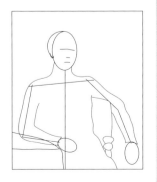

5

Erase the body and arm guidelines. Add small ovals for the eyes. Draw the hairline, cheek, and jaw as shown. Draw the hands.

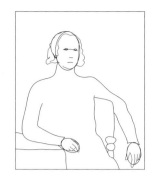

6

Erase the head oval and curve. Draw the collar of Madison's jacket. Draw his shirt using squiggly lines. Add the bottoms of his sleeves. Draw the nose and mouth.

7

Erase the rest of the guides. Draw detail lines around the eyes. Add the eyebrows. Draw lines for the folds in the tablecloth. Add a curtain to the upper left corner. Add detail to the chair arm.

8

Finish with shading. The jacket is very, very dark. The background is dark, too. Use the side of your pencil to shade the background.

Jefferson in France

After the United States became an independent country, Americans needed to establish trade relationships with other countries. In 1784, Congress asked Jefferson to go to France to make trade agreements with European countries. Thomas Jefferson's

Maison Carrée Paris, France

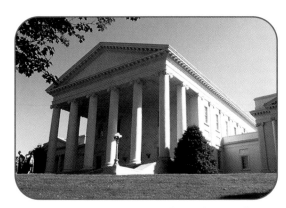

Virginia state capitol, Richmond

only trade agreement, though, was with Prussia. Prussia was a European country that was made up of lands in present-day Germany and Poland.

While in Europe, Jefferson enjoyed its art and music. He was especially interested in the ancient Roman architecture he saw in France and Italy. He liked the Maison Carrée, a Roman temple in Nîmes, France, so much that he later modeled his design for the Virginia state capitol in Richmond after it. During Jefferson's last year in France, the French Revolution began. It lasted from 1789 to 1799. Jefferson sided with the French people, who had revolted against their king and wanted to form a democratic government.

1

Begin your drawing of the Maison Carée by making a large rectangle. Draw a long horizontal line across it. Add the large shape. It is taller on the right side. This will be the front of the building.

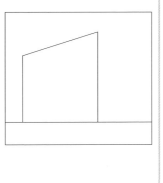

2

Add the lines to the front as shown. These lines make a trapezoid and a triangle with the shape you drew in step 1. Add two lines to make the side of the building.

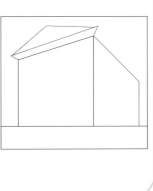

3

Add the lines to the front and side of the building. Draw a short slanted line underneath the front of the building. This will become the edge of the steps.

4

Add another line to the roof, along the side. Draw the shapes underneath the building. Look at the drawing carefully to help you position the shapes.

5

Draw slanting and bumpy horizontal lines to make steps. Draw straight lines on either side of the steps. Draw straight lines in the main building, too.

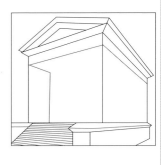

6

Add columns to your building using vertical lines. The tops begin at the uppermost lines you drew in step 5. Draw two more lines above the columns. Add small vertical lines to the left side of the steps.

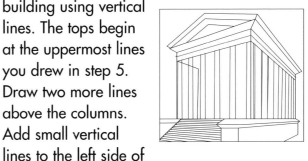

7

Erase extra lines that run through the columns. Draw the tops and bottoms of the columns. Add more lines to the roof. Add a tiny half circle to the very top of the roof.

8

Erase the lines of the columns that go through the tops and the bottoms. Erase the slanted line on the left of the steps so each step has a pointed edge. Finish with shading.

The Louisiana Purchase

In 1801, Thomas Jefferson began the first of his two terms as president of the United States. His most important accomplishment as president was the Louisiana Purchase. In 1802, the Louisiana Territory belonged to France. The city of New Orleans in the Louisiana Territory was important for trade, because it was located on the Mississippi River and the Gulf of Mexico. These waterways were used to ship goods.

In 1803, Jefferson sent James Monroe to France to offer the Emperor Napoleon $2 million for New Orleans. Napoleon offered to sell the entire Louisiana Territory for $15 million. Jefferson approved the sale.

In 1804, Jefferson sent Meriwether Lewis and William Clark to explore this territory. The explorers gave silver peace medals, as shown above, to chiefs of Native American nations they met on their journey. This was meant to show that they were meeting in friendship. The expedition was important, because the explorers described the new territory, which soon drew settlers.

1

Begin your peace medal by drawing three circles as shown.

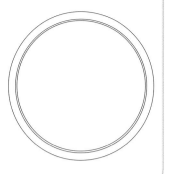

2

Draw the guidelines for where the ax, pipe, and hands will go.

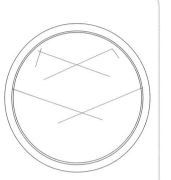

3

Draw the outlines for the ax and pipe. Draw an oval for one hand and a curved line for the other hand. Draw outlines for the arms.

4

Erase the guidelines for the ax and pipe. Erase the straight guidelines for the arms. Draw the lines for the sleeves. Begin to draw the thumb of the hand on the right.

5

Erase the outlines for the arms. Erase the curvy guideline for the hand on the right. Draw the fingers of the hands.

6

Erase the oval guideline for the hand on the left. Draw lines for the fingernails. Write the words "PEACE AND FRIENDSHIP" as shown. Add a flat, narrow oval to the pipe.

7

Add the details to the sleeves. On the left side sleeve, the decoration is made of curved shapes. On the right side sleeve, the decoration is made of curving rounded shapes.

8

Finish with shading. Use the side of your pencil tip to shade the entire medal. Make the areas around the objects darker. Make the palm of the hand darker, too. Nice job!

The University of Virginia

Thomas Jefferson believed that education was very important. For many years Jefferson pushed the Virginia legislature to support free elementary education for children. 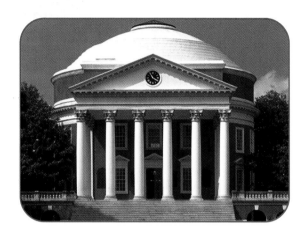 He also wanted the state government to provide money for a public library and a university. After Jefferson's presidency, in 1819, when he was 76, the legislature gave the state $15,000 to begin construction on the University of Virginia. He picked the location for the university in Charlottesville, designed the buildings, and selected the teachers. The university opened with 123 students in 1825.

Jefferson designed the university as an "Academical Village," with a small building for each area of study. At one end of the village is the Rotunda, which served as the university's library. A rotunda is a round building with a dome on top. Jefferson modeled the Rotunda after an ancient Roman temple called the Pantheon. Today the Rotunda is used for events at the university.

1

Begin by drawing a large rectangle. Draw a horizontal line. Draw a line down the middle of the rectangle to the horizontal line. Draw a rectangle on the horizontal line, too.

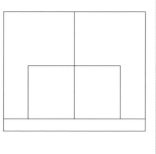

2

Draw two rectangles on top of the center rectangle. Draw the shape with pointing edges. Draw two slanted lines beneath the horizontal line at the bottom. Draw two short horizontal lines.

3

Draw two more short horizontal lines on either side. Draw the roof with slanted lines. Add one long horizontal line and two short vertical lines to the roof. Draw lines for the columns.

4

Erase extra lines. Draw more lines on the roof sections. Draw two rectangles, a line, and a triangle between the center columns. Add the steps. Draw the fence posts on each side.

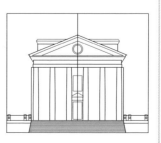

5

Draw windows between the columns. Draw bottoms on the columns. Use curving lines to make the domed section of the building. It is wider and taller than the front part of the building.

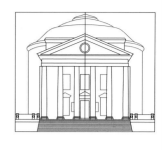

6

Draw a half circle on both sides of the steps. Add a trapezoid on top of each shape. Erase extra lines. Add details to the columns. Add more windows. Draw curvy lines on the sides of the building.

7

Erase extra lines on the sides of the building. Add the windows. Draw smaller columns behind the two outer columns. Erase the extra lines on the columns. Draw the fence. Add details to the triangle.

8

Erase the lines on the sides that run through the windows. Finish with shading. The archways are very dark. The doorway is dark, too. Notice which areas are dark and which are lighter. Nice work!

Jefferson's Legacy

Jefferson died on July 4, 1826, 50 years after the Declaration of Independence was signed. Before he died, Jefferson wrote his epitaph, which reads, "Thomas Jefferson, Author of the Declaration of American Independence, of the Statute of Virginia for Religious Freedom, and Father of the University of Virginia." He was most proud of these three accomplishments and wanted to be remembered for them.

Besides the accomplishments listed on his epitaph, Jefferson served the United States as governor of Virginia, secretary of state, vice president, president, and founder of the Democratic-Republican Party. Jefferson helped stock the Library of Congress when he sold his more than 6,000 books to the government. Jefferson's architectural legacy includes Monticello, the Virginia state capitol, and the University of Virginia, and for this legacy he is called the Father of Our National Architecture. Jefferson is remembered as a man of many talents who served his country well.

1

You are going to draw Thomas Jefferson. Begin by drawing a large rectangle. Draw a guideline for the body. Draw a guide oval for the head.

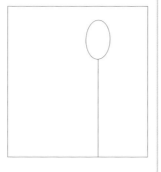

2

Add a curve to the oval. Draw guides for the eyes, nose, and lips. Add lines for the shoulders and arms.

3

Draw a small oval for the ear. It should line up underneath the eye line. Draw a table shape and armchair shape. Draw ovals for the hands.

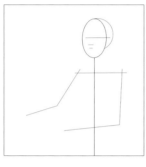

4

Add ovals for the eyes. Draw the lines of the nose and mouth. Draw lines for the cheek and jaw. Draw squiggly lines in the ear oval. Draw the body outline.

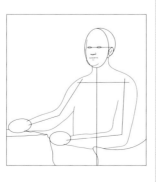

5

Erase the eye, nose, and mouth guidelines. Erase the shoulder and arm guidelines. Draw two circles in the eyes. Draw the hair. Erase part of the ear oval. Draw the lines for the clothes as shown.

6

Erase the head oval and curve. Erase extra lines in the body outline. Add detail to the eyes as shown. Draw eyebrows, the hair ribbon, and the hands. Add detail lines to the furniture. Add the papers under Jefferson's hand.

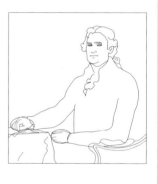

7

Erase the hand ovals. Erase the lines of the table that run through the papers and the part of the clothing that runs through the chair. Add shading. The jacket is very dark. The background is dark, too.

Timeline

1743 Thomas Jefferson is born at Shadwell farm in Virginia.

1757 Jefferson's father, Peter, dies.

1760–1762 Jefferson attends William and Mary College in Williamsburg, Virginia.

1769 Jefferson is elected to the Virginia legislature.

1770 Jefferson begins building Monticello.

1772 Jefferson marries Martha Wayles Skelton.

1776 Jefferson writes the Declaration of Independence.

The Declaration is signed on July 4.

1779–1781 Jefferson serves as governor of Virginia.

1782 Martha Jefferson dies.

1784–1789 Jefferson sent to France to negotiate trade agreements.

1790–1793 Jefferson serves as secretary of state.

1796 Jefferson begins enlarging Monticello and adds the dome.

1797–1801 Jefferson serves as vice president under John Adams.

1801–1809 Jefferson serves as the third president of the United States.

1803 The U.S. government buys the Louisiana Territory from France.

1804–1806 The Lewis and Clark Expedition occurs.

1815 Jefferson sells his library to the government.

1819 Construction begins on the University of Virginia.

1825 The University of Virginia opens.

1826 Thomas Jefferson dies on July 4.

Glossary

academical (a-kuh-DEH-mih-kul) Academic, or related to or connected with a school, especially a college or university.

American Revolution (uh-MER-uh-ken reh-vuh-LOO-shun) Battles that soldiers from the colonies fought against Britain for freedom, from 1775 to 1783.

architect (AR-kih-tekt) Someone who creates ideas and plans for a building.

Bill of Rights (BIL UV RYTS) The first ten amendments to the U.S. Constitution.

committee (kuh-MIH-tee) A group of people directed to oversee or to consider a matter.

Constitution (kon-stih-TOO-shun) The basic rules by which the United States is governed.

Declaration of Independence (deh-kluh-RAY-shun UV in-duh-PEN-dints) An official announcement signed on July 4, 1776, in which American colonists stated they were free of British rule.

democratic (deh-muh-KRA-tik) Having to do with a government that is run by the people who live under it.

designed (dih-ZYND) To have planned the form of something.

epitaph (EH-puh-taf) Words carved in the stone that marks a grave in memory of the one buried there.

inaugurated (ih-NAW-gyuh-rayt-ed) Sworn into office.

legacy (LEH-guh-see) Something left behind by a person's actions.

legislature (LEH-jis-lay-chur) A body of people that has the power to make or pass laws.

orchard (OR-cherd) An area where fruit trees, nut trees, or sugar maples are grown.

pursuit (pur-SOOT) The act of trying to get or to seek something.

revolted (rih-VOLT-ed) Fought against the authority of a government.

united (yoo-NYT-ed) Brought together to act as a single group.

Index

Web Sites

Due to the changing nature of Internet links, PowerKids Press has developed an online list of Web sites related to the subject of this book. This site is updated regularly. Please use this link to access the list:
www.powerkidslinks.com/kgdpusa/jefferson/